R I F F S

DENNIS LEE

RIFFS

BRICK BOOKS

CANADIAN CATALOGUING IN PUBLICATION DATA

Lee, Dennis, 1939-
  Riffs

ISBN 0-919626-65-3

I. Title.

PS8523.E4R5 1993   C811'.54   C93-094567-0
PR9199.3.L44R5 1993

The support of the Canada Council and the Ontario Arts Council is
gratefully acknowledged. The support of the Government of Ontario
through the Ministry of Culture, Tourism and Recreation is also gratefully
acknowledged.

Riffs is a work of fiction.

Cover art by Mary Donlan, 'Freddie's Zig Zag', oil on handmade paper,
18" x 21", 1992.

Typeset in Ehrhardt, printed and bound by The Porcupine's Quill.
The stock is acid-free Zephyr Antique laid.

Brick Books
Box 38, Station B
London, Ontario
N6A 4V3

For Susan, my wife

1

When I lurched like a rumour of want through the networks of plenty,
a me-shaped pang on the lam,
when I ghosted through lives like a headline, a scrap in the updraft,
and my mid-life wreckage was close & for keeps—

    when I watched the
    birches misting, pale spring
    voltage and
    not mine, nor mine, nor mine—

then: a
lady laid her touch a-
mong me, gentle thing, for which I stand still
startled, gentle thing and feel the
ache begin again,
the onus of joy.

2

Nudge of her snuggled head
    against my shoulder,
cool of her flank
    beneath my finger-trails;
all night, all that
    prodigal night at the
tasks of
    passion—
sleep was the place we went,
    as the sun came through.

3

    How
hooked I–
    honey how

    hooked &
horny; hooked and happy-go-
        honking–hey, how

    hooked on your
honey-sweet honey I
    am.

4

clean sheets

hot coffee in mugs

the woman I'm wild for:

    alive in the physical
    world–how come I

    been away so long?

5

Yup, this is how it happens:
you do your half-smile, serious and bantering both,
and right on cue my insides
cave in, they go immaculately wingy . . .

Now it's coming back.
We're apart six hours and there's this
gravitational yank across the city: I would
drive through walls to get near you,
just to be near you . . .

And also the way my body-glow
matches your body-
glow. Or how you flicker with
panic at being held—and I get the empathy bends,
exactly like I'm supposed to . . .

Been a long time.
                    I'd forgotten.

Gimme more.

6

Home-spooked
hotline.   Nobody's li'l number

one.   Big-eyed
radium child on stretched-out scrims of alert—

you could go off in *my*
life? . . . Well of

all

things!

I see you once, and it
happens all over again;
slip me a
hit of that wonky grin and there's rumours of
other–adulterous jostle of
unlived lives, hot possible me's on the prowl.

And then, when we sit down to gab, I get
babel and urspeak.
Sling us some
blues & true con-
cussions, pure jive on a wire: we're pulling
seismic flips and goofball acrobatics–and we
knew it all along!

Aw but when we lie down, it gets
utter. I tumble
head over hormone blur in a
crinkle of selves, sheer
sprong of expanded us:
ow-*ooo!*
We love like a backyard concert of perfect strays.

That's why I wrote you this note.
Wanna hold *your* up-from-lagoons, your
beamed-in-from-Mars bits, too.
Wanna let your many be.
(. . . And how will we
play it? like Bird? like no-trumps? darling, like movies of
speeded-up weather?

8

Ho hum you
said—so soon attuned
to ecstasy.   *Ho*
hum, as if to say,
'Two weeks ago we barely
knew the peaks existed, now they're
rear-view postcard vistas.'
Ho bloody *hum!*—till I cracked the perfect
hubris/satori code: 'Already it's
too good to last   /better
tempt fate fast   /take it for granted and *past* zip *past* zip *past*.'

9

For months before we lay down
it kept going off, it kept going on
like blips & glory traces: sub-
versive inklings of a way—the
way your tact and gags and libidinal gravity
seemed seamless in your body.
I loved the sense of *yes* you moved around in.

To me it meant (like a dare, and I got scared),
'The world didn't have to lose its tang? . . .
That deep, departed hunch, of a life abounding—
that's still for real? . . .
There's plain brown joy on the hoof?'

(And then we laid-me-down. And got to know it.)

They
mock at me, poor
      sensibles–

  '*This* time it's
        gonna hurt!'
But I can't

  change their pygmy
minds; sweet splash of
        dynamite, just

  graze on
me & you, the way we do, in
    late-20th-

century eden entry high.
                (. . . Rare old
    rendezvous on earth.

      Why else are we here?)

11

  When you present
    your body and being and
utterly, bright-eyed
      companion–

and when we go deep into
        one another's eyes, and the
    swim of communion is
ancient,
        ancient and grave—

or when you speak, not just of
        love but of
impediments to loving, and even that

    serious caution inflames me: delicate
                scrunch of your shoulders,
        probe of your moral concern—

        how can such gifts undo me?
                Why does my system declare
        Ha!
They'll never get out of paradise alive?

12

But she's gone—she's an
    ocean away, and

what is she
    dreaming?

13

Sweet christ, you are
lovely–over & over:

tonight I can nearly
taste it.   Track of your hopscotch your

quicksilver
trace in my

mind; wry bracketed giggle,
that triggers an ache at the

core; and over & over, new
sister & stranger your born-again

flow on my
tongue . . .

Why aren't you here?

14

So I'll cook some
thump & witness, raise a
bumper car in the dictionary:

make up a real-
life us,
at play in the garden of words–

     remember?

Not that we were good enough.
But there was this new and, yes foreknown astonishment:
somehow we were being actively permitted to live in our skins.

15

Those perfect
conversations, with their lazy
clarity uncoiling . . .

Skin still homing to
skin, confederate across a
roomful of chatter . . .

And fit of a life to a
lifetime: sedulous, incredulous, and OK downright
smug as we
basked around the block, two nerds in a blurt of summer . . .

Doesn't anybody
know? we asked—not about us, about
acres of luminous storefronts, *camouflaged as storefronts,*
the sky in drag as sky, as blue as itself,
                                        and,
free for the taking,
all dirt & secrets of newly-indigenous earth.

Plus our non-stop, gut-bucket grins.

Heaven *con carne.*

16

Hot po-
tato momma, got you in my

mouth all night.
Absenty

lady–
land o'

livin, I could pay my
rent all year & *still* owe dues.

17

Some kinda
stunts & wonders? Hocus-
focus? Hot cross

nerve ends?
Come on c'mon nice
lady, we ain't got all

lifetime! . . . Indefatigably-adored one:

please to
appear on the sheet right now, called up by
succulent, shrink-wrapped, wholly-refundable me.

18

    Eerie
articulations of

        love-
space:

        delicate
angles:

        arousal.

Will I
        trace this

deft a
        space upon your
body?

Would you be
                    here?

19

Wal, acey deucey
        trey divide−
I'm a guy
        with a fine wide-eyed

lady freckles too &
 squirms when she
feels good, I feel so
 good just

doin aw
 shucks
tricks an she's
 SOFISTIKATED!

20

Hey honey,
 it
sizzles.

Come closer, wanna
 see your
eyeballs roll!

Wanna
 tell ya
things . . .

Don't like it, just
 don't come
in here—y'

  hear?

21

Capo and
fret, the
comical flesh
arrangements—flexed by
what rare
air, what gifted melody trace?

22

    One thing
weird is,
       blowing

highwire struts of be–
      bop-a-
longing for

    lady in her moves, don't talk this
way—patrician
      dancer, *no-*

body's
      trick;
and has calm, and yes an olden chastity and whose

    pleasure is
classic, and breathes.

23

Six weeks of
plonk & longing?

riffs of
rendezvous with you?

I'm here to coin new nerve-ends, fashion an
icon habitation, name of

be-when-my-reason-for-
being-is-snatched-away . . .

    while you
    think some things through.

24

           Oh babe!
      when you come home, there'll be
        mountains of hot patootie:
    bow-ties and ice-cream,
  could be a big parade.
And speeches—aw honey the
      speeches will curl your ego;
    talkin bout
      lady of riffs &
      backrubs, my lady of nowhere—said, the
  damsel of cro-mignonne and the
      life we're gonna lead
    (big changes, chérie: *beeg* decisions)—

      when you come home.

25

'Hello . . . hullo? Yes it's
me—no no, there's no

problem, I just want to
change your life. So

look if you're
free tonight, could you

live with me?' . . .

    (Come quick and we'll install

wet dreams in arcady, little donner &
vixen we'll rearrange the

continental mindset as
fallout & dandruff, and

oh,
by the way

could you
please be my baby—my

baby, *my* baby—
tonight?

I said I was
'happy'? . . . OK: so I
      lied.

      The forcible re-
construction of a
      life,

      caused by (woman, *deli-*
cado) the grave
      assertion of your

      pride, your need, your cells, your self-
donations in the dark–that is
      not, re-

      peat *not*
summed up by
      'happy.'

      Try,
terror. Try, *what I was born for.* Try, *whiff of*
      zero at the

      core, in this claiming
sluice of utter
      joy . . .

      Try,
how are we meant to live?

27

But if I
got un-

lucky once—meaning, if jiggers of neuron
delight flashed non-stop thru my

system yet I
had no hope of you, your

lissome stretch in bed, your
wit your gab your *areté* your life-on-the-line

embrace, sweet lean to graciousness your
curve in the mind your melt your fathoming goodness, gift of

wayward grace in a
giggle—if, I say if I

got unlucky for an hour and
lost you for a lifetime, one long

scan of dead
tomorrows if I

had no
hope of you . . .

28

Hey funny thing, I had this
dream I dreamt you
came back here,

alive in my arms—not even your spiffy
clothes—but then I
woke and the sheet was drenched, it had loved-in

holes in it . . .

29

Will pass your place.
Will think of us in
two-tone pandemonium,
performing the belly the breast,
performing the stations,

referring all calls to the wizard of waste not
want.   Your waist: your sultry waist.
My stupid want.

30

Multifarious dodos:
notably extinct—

gangs of ex-
es copped their snuff & split—
nobody wants to be nobody—

I just say I know you are fallible & gun-shy and still we could

occupy one planet

and look in tomorrow's mirror and start to brush *one two one two*

31

The angels'
cure for when they miss someone *very* bad is
    malt whiskey.

    'Dja
know that?
    I never knew that.

    Found out
my own way, special,
    just since you

    went away and to–
night at 2:48 a.m. I am
    practising up being an angel twinkle twinkle mud

32

Awright,
        jubilee:
le's pull off the
        mirror.

        You're looking like late-night
heaven.
        You're looking like rain.
You lookin like four on the floor & I thought I was hitching.

I thought we were quicksilver, now you're a
        ten-minute
coffee stop.

33

    Hey, should I
talk
    sociology?

    when where what how who?

All I
    want, woman, is
crawl up your left nostril & snuff it for keeps in sexual asthma heaven.

34

Music of
    methodist forebears.

Flesh inheritance.

I say these dreadful things for
    what I got left, I got rites of
ache & legacy.

35

So I'm too
    'obsessive,'
        huh? Too 'wired to your moods'? . . .

Tonight our
    spats come back.   (Oh yeah:
    Return of the Wandering Spats.)

And sure: you cute, me
    addictive–but honey you
            ain't seen nothin yet!

I got heartaches in real-time. Got this
            separation from hell,
    guilt with my kids, I got

two friends dead in a year my
        gallant parents soon and the nights, these
    plummeting dipso nights plus the

planet's shot–you're all I got left to
            hang on to.   You bet I
        hang on hard.

36

                And not just that.
                        Most days, I'm
                not obsessed *enough*.   For the
        world sustains–it must!–a pour of
                joy.   Somewhere, sanely past
                        wishing, it
            rides into phase with the
    news of its own largesse.
                And bids us partake, calling,
                    Hey, last
            chance to
            dance!
    last shot at flesh and danger!
                        For years I felt that hunger.
            Yet always what I

ran from was the hunch, my well-planned
life the barricade—until two years ago I busted up my
life, to instigate a
blitz of deeper presence.
Just touch it, before I'm gone.

Since then, I'm a
freelance lightning rod,
hot for *tremendum*.
Since then I tote the yen like a sanctified growth—but shit, how
rarely I sustain it . . .
C'mon, *you* know this stuff,
you're holy locus.
Don't say I'm 'too intense,' you jerk: you triggered grace-with-cleavage.

37

Honey, it's
soo heroic:

'hot for
tremendum.'

All that leaves out is,
the drone of the rest of my life.

All it leaves out is
the doldrums of making a buck,

daily ego de-
bris, those non-stop misfires—oh

babe!—with a bevy of
red-hot maidens, bad trance of this

killer civilisation, yeah,
the blahs the yays the blues the yack-yack-yack;

all it leaves out is the stoopit miles of missing you—
the (hi, maw!) muddle of me.

38

When you're up to yr
homburg in
hopeless, & the

damsel is not here—

what merrie cheer? zip zip no goddam cheer:

just
DIT-DAT-DOTs of biological/
ontological urgency—

pages of empties . . .
late-night lady reprise.

39

Pen-
ultimate lady, alive—sweet

skin and sesame:
why do we ever rub con-

tours, if not to conjure
shapes of what we aren't and

crave to be? . . .
Touching you I am

meat & pronto, I lounge in the chutzpah of
flesh; then woozy with

laughter and midnight and
caring, pure

carnal
panache—you, you, you in your frabjous parade—

how should I
reach for more?

Yet always behind you (this is
why I shy away), barely be-

yond you
is

nothing at all . . .
Lady,

do not be offended when I
go there.

40

All the left-out
corners,

faeces of living, the
lint:

show me a riff with straight-up ejection & I want

those in too,
and count on your body to help.

41

Inch by
inch by inkling: niche by hunch.

Rock at my temples; sheer drop; fingertip
grips & a piss-poor attendance record in the daily adhesive world.

42

    My
comrade of the
     ineffable:

    let me take you
down to
     logos:

    pre-
logos,
     where

    stones stone,
light lights,
     hurt things & people hurt and go on hurting.

43

    Can't hold them together:—

We two were given to emerge
to deep-down here and now;
it was plain & quirky, as
rooted in daylight as grass,
bright with its own green sheen and
when we go, our going will not diminish it—

    And here on the planet, what news?
    A single scene:
    that 8-month child in Chile, electricity
    up her vagina; the sergeant is

flicking the button; he waits, flicking & flicking to
make the parents inform but they *cannot*, they
never heard those names;
as well he knows.
                              And
again: that 8-month child in Chile, the—

Vertiginous thoughtface.
Almost the heart goes missing.
Yet if I
deny the slaughterhouse world—
or if I deny the luminous presence—
something goes numb at the core.

 But open-to-both is
 mayhem—
 nothing beside that child's—yet
 falling apart with static and
 origin /incommensurable jangling /what is, and what is.

44

Barely, be
mouth.

Mouth to
loathing:

thrills in the
abbatoir . . .

Mouth to
jags of

awkward, un-
prompted joy . . .

Be mouth, and after that and what about us I
do not know.

45

If not for you,
I would be homeless in my going through the world.
It does not
attach you, but I have no good
person to lie down in—saving
yourself,
and the persuasion to.
If you hold to our jointure, I will be
strengthened in the holding that I do.

46

Your voice on my machine—and
I'm totalled, I'm
totally totalled again.

    '. . . So
    it's me—Miz
    Plonk & Longing: remember
    the wet wet witch of the West?'

Oh
    babe, do I ever!
My heart so full of you . . .
But *click!*, and you stopped.

Doxymoronic
darling, li'l breaded klutzlet:
get back here yesterday!
Gonna amorize you over 25 years, got some
full frontal loving to spare;

long distance love to spare,
from an ache with ears.

47

Take me again—
    suite of longing, suite of

lies and
    take me again.

48

Sweetheart: you gave me the
gift of ecstatic be-

longing, which is a
real live

piece of
shit . . .

There you go—haring through
Europe with that

hemorrhoidal
twit, while I sit here hot for heaven &

re-runs on
flat earth and fucking im-

peccably up at
what pas-

ses for a
life? . . .

Belle beautiful lady; cardiac
angel; my

cystine madonna—thanks a hairy
cluster!

May you rot in Buffalo.

49

      But was I in
love with you, or with the
      image of your

      layabout love-
play, by
      bed-

      lamps magni-
fied on the
      ceilings of Literature?

      (. . . Gawd I said, I don't want
Literature I just want
      you &

      changed the ribbon.

50

It is
      possible:

you could be words and tomorrow—
      colony

homage, *aere perennius* and you still yodelling back,
      'No, no, let them

eat *my* cake if they're empty,' as your
      figurehead recedes into red-shift anthology legends.

51

Smelting head foundries of ozone gravity breakage I
ached in a space and heard Keep keep keep

coming like something in flames
coming like nothing

coming like words are what a man could burn and burn in, and for keeps.

52

We swam into
paradise easy . . .

That was in the flesh . . .

Now it's
clobber & slop and
drag the jubilee hunch through a
busted language, you not
here.

53

Why else do I squat like a rain-
bow bruise in the night, arch-
ing in absence to you? . . .

It is for
lust. And
not just you!
             The
world that lay in blitz and bits stood

singlified to our ken.   And if I
let the damn thing go, that
itch of a glory norm–

how would I breathe, in non-ecstatic time?

54

Three weeks.
No call.   No news.

Whadja think–I'm blind or something?
You're choosing *him:*
junk male incarnate.

And wherever you are tonight–
half-sloshed, skirt hiked, on your
back in some famous alley–
you've made your choice.

You had a crack at
sheer valhalla overdrive.

Now go piss up a rope.

55

Okay, I knew it was wrong.
            Over and over I asked you,
'What about him?
                  doesn't it bother you?'

                  But *oh no*—
      it was
            two different things, you said, it was
god knows what you said, you had all the answers . . .

                  Moon come soon.
            Big old moon like a
                  plate of dogsick, and honey I'm tired,
                  tired—I am so utterly

      tired of this slimy ribbon of
                  lies, wound round my
            head, my
                  shame my

too-long life to come . . .

                  Let's kill this now.

56

All
    fall, desiring
       desire, I
          magnified her name.
This one is for lies.

      This one is for
  old-time-cheating lies. For
        A=D=U=L=T=E=R=Y lies.   This goes out for
101 Lessons in How to Lie to Yourself–meaning, first, those
             oinks of eternal troth.
     For the lie of *her-husband-doesn't-have-soul,-so-it's-okay.*

     And on and on, the lie of a
        love supreme when we
made it *in toto* six times, the lie of a
           love made true by danger, memory lie of her
       exquisite alleycat grace the lie of these
      all-night
    riffs & jackoffs this goes out for
     months of a life gone missing, for
          scotch black russian cinzano this one is for
          cowardice lies, for
      hold-me and *save-me* and *us–*

57

    Roadkill love.
  Reality meathook ruptures.

      You know I
    put my life in your keeping.

Jugular mercy.
Flick of your barbwire caress.

Wrongly, I guess–but
you told me you'd hold me forever.

Venom & blues.

58

Fact: it was
wrong from the start.
Our treks through
plenary skin and vistas, the quantum
blastoff to lovers' clear –
those were
snotty renditions of soulful.
Furtive.   Self-serving.   A lie.

But if I gain
beatitude galore, and lose the gift of
moral discernment,
how real are my rarefied highs?
If I teem with ecstatic
fulfilment but, bye-bye centre:
what good is my life?

Deep source, dire
origin: my
swarm of thoughts is
busywork, and what is real

                    exerts its steady terror.
          The words are so much yack.
                              I happen in the spaces.
    But when my life goes mute again, tonight,
              I have no place to be,
                              except your deep,
                    except your stark,
                         except your stern.

59

     Maybe *you-and-me* was a lie.
But that big old easy place, where the

     preternatural authority
flared out and, wham, it was

     simply *a*
man and a woman:

     that was
deeper than you-and-me . . .

     And okay, it's us that got mugged.
And a

     lark and
a wrench and a lifetime.

     But also, that
space of epochal

being is
shaped like home (even if

what? and *where did it go?*
are past my ken).   And now, though I

may not stay
bonded to you, by

reason of unclean union, still I
will not stop homing to

home.

60

It was bad.   Bad! It got
        bad, and
honey I'm sorry: I
                lost the beat.
                That stuff was garbage.

But listen, your letter just came—and
we're gonna make it! got
                too much to lose . . .

So let's go
back to the good part again;
        nothing is pure.

Back to
            he plus she, and
electric ever after—please, back to our

                    tantric
        buzz, that eros/
            lobotomy smorgasbord.

61

There were
coals of noel, hot bother & jeez, don't wanna

grab you for numinous stand-ins but honest to
edges got charred, fucken

wings half came off—
thought I was crocked & goners.

. . . Think I'd let go of
you, and heaven, now?

62

        Clear tracings in
empty space:

        from silence,

        nothing to
words to back to back to silence . . .

I could go
drunk into

jive-time, the
emptiness, these halo lady

tracings.

63

Look maw—no mind, and
I can

stick to the stony face of
nothing,

nothing-&-
you, and inch a-

head for one
more chomp on the root of *is*.

64

Stir me again.

I cd be hoisted *how* high, I cd be
god in a handcart: BLEEP.

Even the speechlessest rockface deigns to utter its pendant climbers.

65

One week to go: come
soonest.
Have walked some
planks since you been gone and now
would love to walk straight up the plank to
you arriving.
'Take *that*,' I'd say, and hand you what has
happened since you left but I would
take it back awhile, lie down and
breathing slow beside you hope to
ease your eyelid stress and coming home.

66

Burning thru
altitudes of lifetime:
atmosphere very thin, me
very too. Fuel for outward, low—
back, a farce.

Signal if you are receiving this, otherwise ciao.

67

There is a pure
        over-
load, & it

        copes
w/
        modernity . . .

I want that. I also want
    chaucer and
water.

68

Just now I thought to your
doorway, you opened we
stood stock still in mind.
You were going to say, You *did* come but we
headed through the hall and
stood in the eerie surround—it was
locked, recalcitrant wholeness,
so shattering I felt
relieved we could not speak; we were almost
unmade to be together; we did not know,
Should things start here, or end? were we even a
ping on the face of silence?

69

       So now you want me dead.
             I
   get the message.

        For months you had me
      hung by the heels and
       dripping;

            now it's
   haul out the
      guts, & flush.

So darling–Happy
Returns! must be some
anniversary or other in the

ghoul crusade.
Maybe the first time you
skewered me with your laugh. Or that deadly initial

I love you,
at dusk, in High Park. Or the soon-to-be-never-
forgotten climax when you

dumped me, you
dumped me, you
came back today and you

dumped me, bitch and
congrats!
(And

thanks for the killer putdowns.
You butted me out . . .

Now I get to lick the ashtray.)

70

All that stuff it was monkey-grip jive your mean mean mind
who saw your chance and slid in fast you came for manhood
took it shook it trashed my self-respect–but you know I
never did like your body,
never those porridge thighs the spider scrawl around your eyes

right right every midnight wail about your body shape was true

those moves you made in bed old *Joy of Sex* retreads, my friends all used
    to yuck it up when I described them

and there was never a 'sacred place' it was fake I winced at the slobbery
    gash of your mouth when you came

who was my hardon for living you made me crazy but I never loved
    your breasts

never drank your freefall mind didn't give me a buzz that talkie jive you
    really done me,

screwyou screwyou never craved your roadblock thighs your rehash
    moves in bed never did care for your flirt your flounce your paeans
    your mean mean knockout mind

71

'Please,
don't forget me.'

. . . Please don't *forget* you?

Oh right: you were just about to
slip my foolish mind.
Thanks for the memo.

    (But tell you what.
    Stir the knife around—to the
    left now, a little bit lower—

    and you'll get not just the heart but also the heights the pits the
        drizzling shits & fun fun fun on Yonge Street Saturday night.)

72

Revved with
contagion, mumbling my

other names and re-
peat: Don't *know* this guy, just some

oddball goof wandered in for the sandwiches,
    for the body braille,
    for the heap big miniaturized cosmos itsy largesse.

[Stop all wired systems STOP.
Abandon all forms of pig-out epiphany addiction.]

73

SKID skid, dopey li'l
juggernaut;
Molotov sidecar momma, wrench me a frog.

If you got happiness tablets throw some out the window way down
    opposite side.

74

Hey I scraped the
guywire limit—been so
high so long I don't know low from Lassie.
Ecstatic on empty.

(& if you are leastwise interested, think to
salute as I shoot straight past you CLONK go push down brown-eyed
    daisies

75

        Goin t'
            psych-
    o whiteout count-
        ry, gonna

meet my baby there—

        She make a space I
            be there: nerve-
    end wipeout, wired for sound—

Cash on my head, came barrelling thru off-
side splendours; fetched up
quaint in a dollop of hell.

        Humans cannot live here.

76

the stupid artillery of stars

moon a cold car-crash

snow piled high on the lawn and
me here sweating

face down in it,
fondling her name, and

puking   puking

77

Gone, it is
gone.   And I
make myself a lie, carrying on about it.

Time was I felt
clear meltdown in the flesh.
Gone: it is gone.

I could not hold to it gently enough; my
finger-clench blackened; the bruise.
                              Well, now I still turn, turn,
turn myself on in the dark—but what is to be done with

this pittance my leftover life?

78

From one half-wasted by
bourgeois heaven & hell, and some tonight
would crawl 5 miles to be (mildly) discomfited so,
so taut is their agony—

say it:
whom do I pray to?
what do I centrally serve?

the 41 years of a selfish, directionless life,
halfway to goners now,
with its jerkoff highs, no right to even blaspheme . . .

Scour me. Scour me, deepness, before I die.

79

Blood on
    behemoth.

Tracts of sheer
    unness.

Abyss and
    interludes.

I did that thing, I just can't walk home straight.

80

Egg-
shell

a-
live-o.

Still, a
live &

living live-
o . . . Just

to be.

Piecemeal-

ly. Pang in bare
potency.

81

Get up eat fruit brew coffee,
do work see friends lie down.

Squeegeed in moments.
I am being squeegeed in detox moments. And all the

highs I can no longer afford—
irony, booze, hot transcendental crushes—

still throb like absentee limbs.

Get up. Do work. Lie down.

82

Rockface
        hallelujah.

Thought-
        high
emergence of

        foothold:

faithful

                : phrase.

83

No, please, not again:

Your voice on my machine—

and I'm
back in the heartspace of
lonely . . .

But the season is
over: that season of
flawless idolatry wank.

84

Byword, &
byword.
In beach-flesh

depths are
beings, under stone.

Us too. I barely shifted the silt of a comma.

85

Am going soon, but meanwhile I can hear
what mortals care for,
instep and desire.
Tell me what you cherish, won't
just walk; give me lifetime,
not renege.
I have no other use. Living I flubbed.
But mouth to mouth I could sometimes ache into words.

86

There is an
                    indoors of the selfsame, which
        calls to a straitened heart.

(And hunger.

        Hunger.)

87

        In her . . . And
then we were home.

        Our
breath bunched, the shudder—us

        twined—of
(and if the) desire and the

    planet
go on, the maybe tomorrows and

      missing her   bad, though our

names and are

        (written

wind

88

The dolphins of need be-
lie their shining traces.
Arcs in the air.

They do not mean to last. One
upward furrow, bright & the long disappearance,

as though by silver fiat of the sea.

Author's Note

In jazz, the term 'riff' has changed in meaning over time. It now refers most commonly to a brief melodic figure improvised by a soloist.

An early version of *Riffs* appeared in the winter 1982 issue of *Descant*. It was written with aid from the Scottish Arts Council and the Canada Council, and benefited from the editorial eye of Donna Bennett. In making this version, I've continued to pick the brains of a dozen long-suffering friends, who know my gratitude. Jan Zwicky's editing has been invaluable.

Special thanks to Walter Marion Jacobs, and to J.S. Bach's *Unaccompanied Cello Suites*.

*

Where a page break falls in the middle of a poem, it coincides with a stanza break except at the bottom of pages 27, 32, 42 & 49.

Dennis Lee was born in Toronto in 1939. He has written *Civil Elegies*, *The Gods*, and a number of collections of children's poetry.